About this book

This step-by-step guide is a record of my specialist support work with a Key Stage 2 pupil with dyslexia who showed very good visual-spatial skills. Alfie's natural gravitation towards patterns and problems that can be worked out using spatial thinking strategies provided both of us with continuous rewarding outcomes. Today, he is a confident maths learner equipped with strategies to recall all times tables. Flash cards and re-writing times tables facts (and any form of rote learning by repeating whole multiplication facts) had never worked for Alfie because of weak sequential working memory. In contrast, by meaningfully engaging his brain with novel times table tricks, Alfie discovered a new way, using patterns that were previously hidden or jumbled up in his mind. Through the use of fingers, his brain created brand new clusters of strong neural networks to support his memory for times table facts. The tricks worked as memory triggers for Alfie.

Of course the tricks are not an end in themselves; they are only ever useful if they are practised and over-practised. Confident recall of times table facts frees the individual's cognitive processing power to engage in mathematical problem solving. Not having a strategy for basic times tables can be a handicap to anyone with otherwise sound underlying numerical ability, as is often the case in dyslexia. Those with impaired mathematical skills, such as learners with dyscalculia, may find that times tables tricks are the only strategy, the last resort, to ever get correct answers in formal maths assessments.

This guide is for learners of all ages who:

– have tried (without success) rote learning methods based on repetition of whole multiplication facts
– enjoy active learning through discovery and experience
– have gaps in their times tables knowledge
– need fast and foolproof strategies to recall times tables in formal assessments, particularly timed ones
– may have a specific learning difficulty (SpLD), such as dyslexia, dyscalculia and ADD/ADHD

The book works by:

– helping over-learn secure reference points in the times tables, from which more tricky facts can be worked out.

– validating alternative methods for learning times tables. Rote learning **does not work for everyone**. Using fingers is not a sign of cheating. For those who are self-conscious, the book's *preferred* (but not exclusive) way of using fingers is gentle tapping on the table (instead of raising hands) to avoid attracting attention to oneself.

– offering multisensory instruction methods that help counteract the effects of weak sequential working memory and poor long-term memory for number facts.

How to use this book

– Only practise one 'trick' at a time (until its recall becomes fully automatic) before moving on to the next one. This is to avoid becoming confused or overwhelmed.

– Once you've learned a trick, practise it as often as you can: later the same day and in the following days and weeks. Share it with other people; use it as a family, class, or party trick. Test yourself during quiet times at home.

– The book doesn't need to be read from cover to cover. You can dip in and out, starting with the trick that looks most appealing or makes the most sense to you.

– Different brains respond differently to maths methods. Don't worry if some tricks don't make sense straight away. Leave them for now, enjoy another trick, then come back to it later. It's fine to learn only some tricks in this book.

lidia.stanton@icloud.com   https://uk.linkedin.com/in/lidiastanton   https://facebook.com/dyslexiaideas

Copyright @ 2019 Lidia Stanton
Illustrations @ 2019 Lidia Stanton
All rights reserved.
Individual pages may be copied for personal use only.
ISBN: 9781671538061

Skip-counting on fingers
x 2, x 5 and x 10

Counting on fingers is not cheating – particularly when learning times tables – whether you do it by folding or unfolding, or gently tapping your fingers.

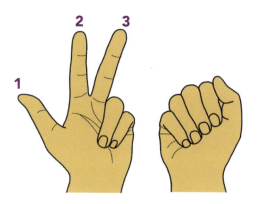
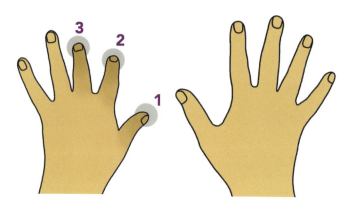

People around you are less likely to notice if you're silently tapping on the desk.

2	5	10
4	10	20
6	15	30
8	20	40
10	25	50
12	30	60
14	35	70
16	40	80
18	45	90
20	50	100
22	55	110
24	60	120
26	65	130

Our brains like patterns, which is why skip-counting seems so easy for the x 2, x 5 and x 10 tables.

Practise skip-counting in 2s, 5s and 10s until you can do it really fast and without mistakes.

To **make it fun**, skip-count while:
-- walking the stairs up and down
-- jumping on a trampoline
-- hopping on pavement slabs
-- tapping fence rails
-- sorting out cereal pieces, buttons, toothpicks, or even cutlery items
-- tapping on library book spines
-- eye-spying white, silver, red, blue or black cars in a car park.

To work out 2 x 7, skip-count in 2s on fingers **7 times**.

2, 4, 6, 8, 10, 12, 14
1 2 3 4 5 6 7

2 x 7 = 14

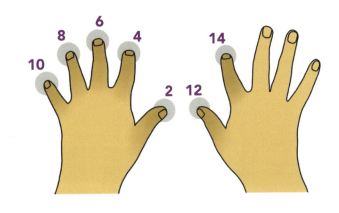

To work out 5 x 6, skip-count in 5s on fingers **6 times**.

5, 10, 15, 20, 25, 30
1 2 3 4 5 6

5 x 6 = 30

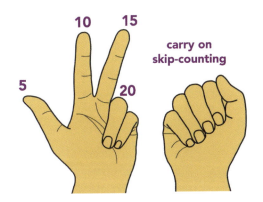

carry on skip-counting

Skip-counting in 2s, 5s and 10s gives us **reference points** in the big grid of times tables. Just find the nearest fact that you know (in yellow) and work from there.

x	1	2	3	4	5	6	7	8	9	10	11	12
1	1	2	3	4	5	6	7	8	9	10	11	12
2	2	4	6	8	10	12	14	16	18	20	22	24
3	3	6	9	12	15	18	21	24	27	30	33	36
4	4	8	12	16	20	24	28	32	36	40	44	48
5	5	10	15	20	25	30	35	40	45	50	55	60
6	6	12	18	24	30	36	42	48	54	60	66	72
7	7	14	21	28	35	42	49	56	63	70	77	84
8	8	16	24	32	40	48	56	64	72	80	88	96
9	9	18	27	36	45	54	63	72	81	90	99	108
10	10	20	30	40	50	60	70	80	90	100	110	120
11	11	22	33	44	55	66	77	88	99	110	121	132
12	12	24	36	48	60	72	84	96	108	120	132	144

How do the **reference points** work in practice? Let's have a tricky example: 6 x 7. If you can't remember 6 x 7, skip-count 5 x 7 and add one more 7.

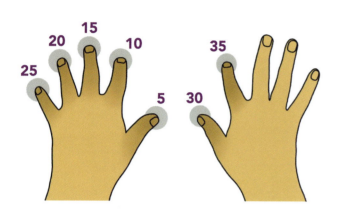

6 x 7 = __

5, 10, 15, 20, 25, 30, 35
1 2 3 4 5 6 7

5 x 7 = 35

Add an extra 7:

35 + 7 = 42

6 x 7 = 42

I start skip-counting with my left thumb, but it's not the only way to do it. Do what feels 'right' for you, as it will also be 'right' for your brain.

Mnemonics (memory triggers)

7 x 7 = 49
Servant, servant! Faulty line!
Seven times seven is forty nine.

4 x 4 = 16
A four by four is a mean machine.
I'm going to get one when I'm 16.

8 x 8 = 64
I ate and I ate and I fell on the floor.
Couldn't get up till I was 64.

OR **8 x 8 = 64**
I ate and I ate till I was sick on the floor.
Eight times eight is sixty four.

9 x 9 = 81
Line to line helps Katie plan.
Nine times nine is eighty one.

7 x 8 = 56
Line them up and that is it!
Seven times eight is fifty six.
5 6 7 8

Now come up with your own rhymes.
They don't have to be perfect. They just have to work for you!

Times tables on fingers
x 6, x 7, x 8 and x 9

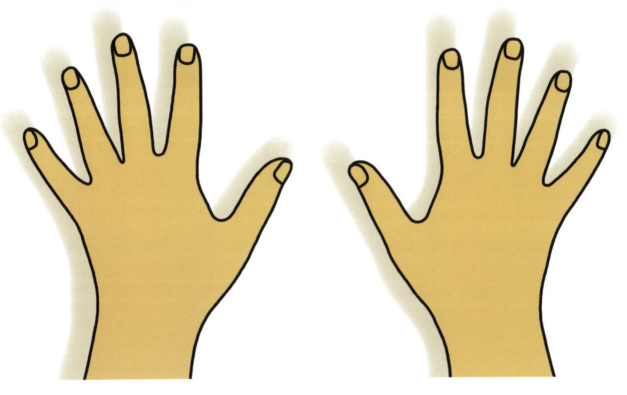

Place your hands over a table without touching the hard surface. Now give each finger a number, as in the pattern below. Practise remembering the positions.

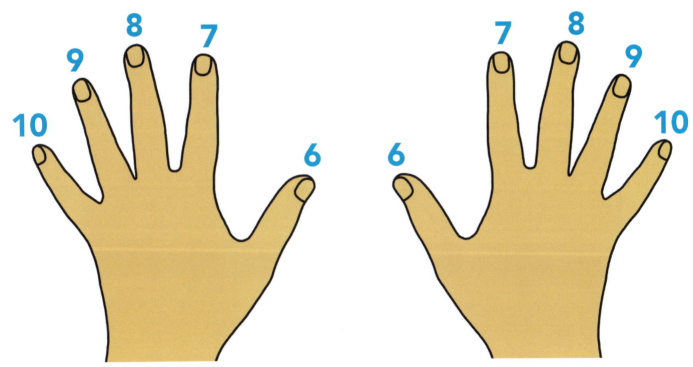

7 x 8 = __

Find fingers 7 and 8 and press the two fingers down on the table.

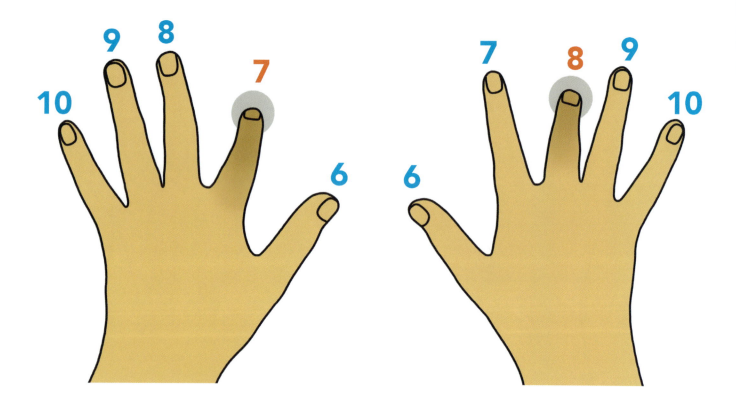

Now press down all the fingers between 7 and 8.

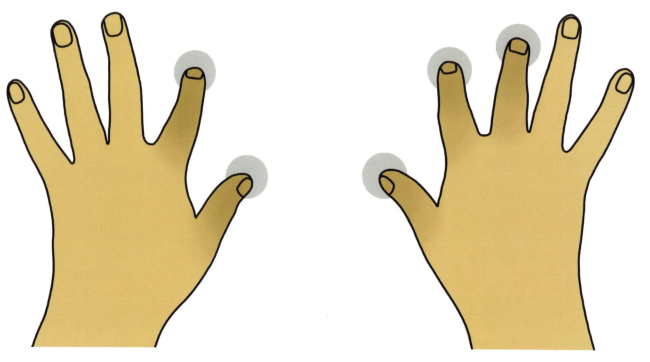

These are your TENS.
How many tens have you got in front of you?

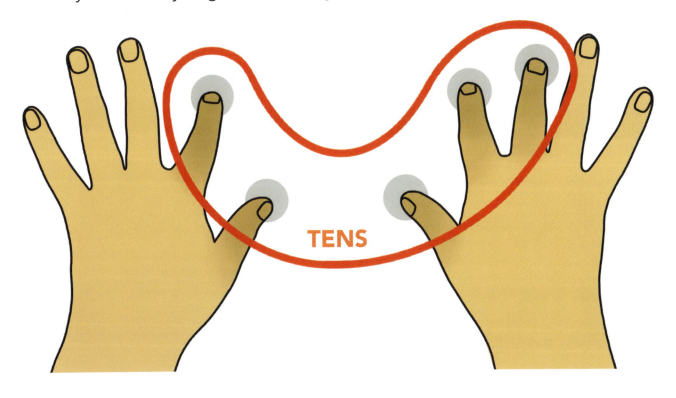

There are 5 tens: 5 x 10 = 50
We will come back to the 50. But what about the remaining fingers in the air?

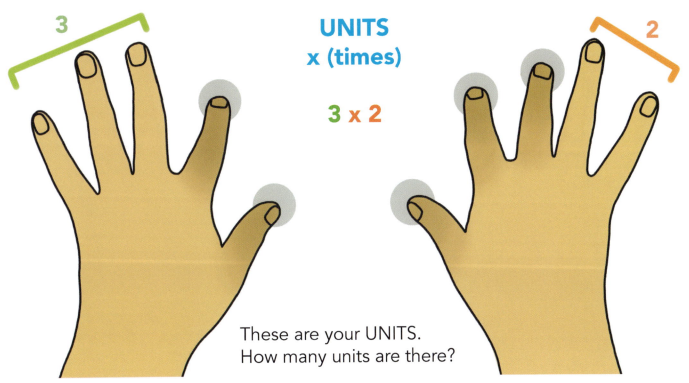

These are your UNITS.
How many units are there?

I have 3 fingers in the air on one hand and 2 on the other. I will multiply them.

3 x 2 = 6

Now, I'll add the TENS (50) and UNITS (6) together.

TENS + UNITS

50 + 6 = 56

The answer to the question 7 x 8 = __ is

7 x 8 = 56

Here's another example:

8 x 8 = __

Have you found 8 and 8 on both hands and pressed them down on the table?

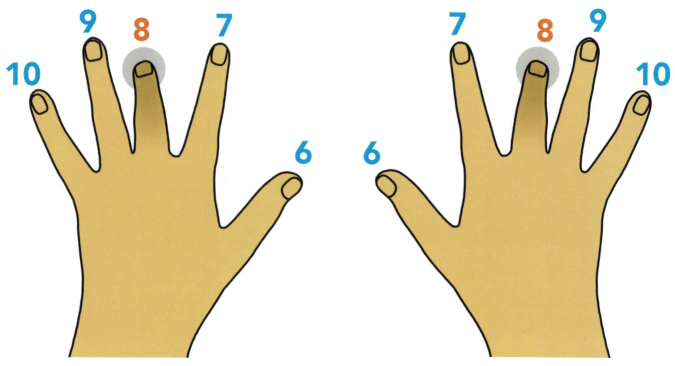

Have you pressed down all the fingers between 8 and 8?

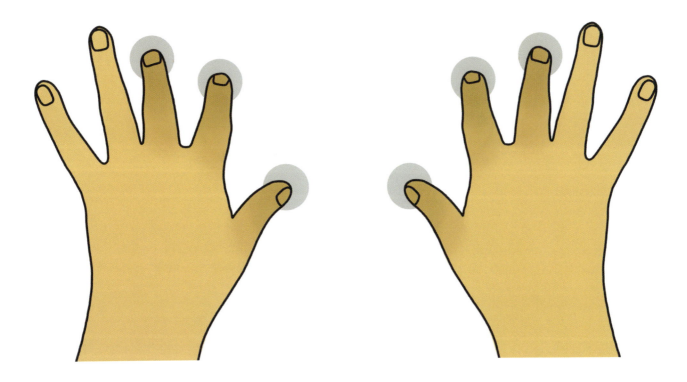

How many TENS have you got?

Six. Three on one hand, and 3 on the other.

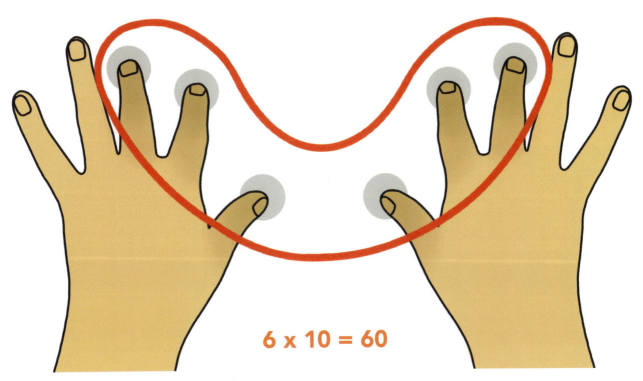

6 x 10 = 60

How many UNITS have you got in the air?

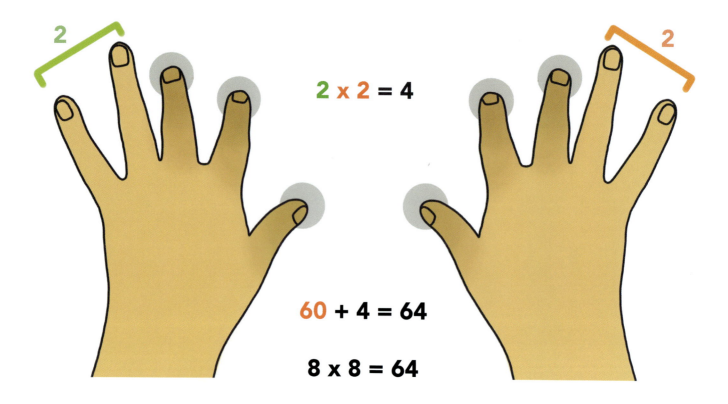

2 x 2 = 4

60 + 4 = 64

8 x 8 = 64

Don't forget you're always adding TENS and UNITS together. Have a look at this example:

6 x 6 = __

Have you pressed down the 6 and 6 fingers? How many TENS have you got between the 6 and 6 fingers? Only two (2).

2 x 10 = 20

How many UNITS are there in the air? Four on one hand, and 4 on the other.

4 x 4 = 16   which is the same as
              1 TEN and 6 UNITS

TENS + UNITS

20 + 16 = 36
               or
               20 + 10 = 30
               30 + 6 = 36

Times tables on fingers
x 9

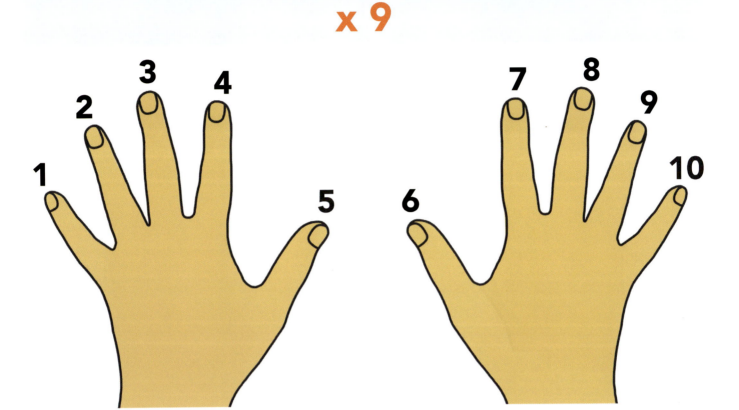

There's another way to do the x 9 table on fingers. And the finger numbers are much easier to remember. Simply count 1 to 10 from left to right.

5 x 9 = ___

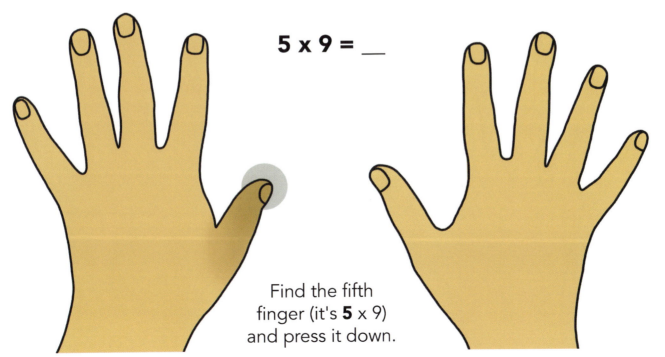

Find the fifth finger (it's **5** x 9) and press it down.

Now count the number of fingers BEFORE the pressed one -- these are your TENS, and AFTER -- these are your UNITS.

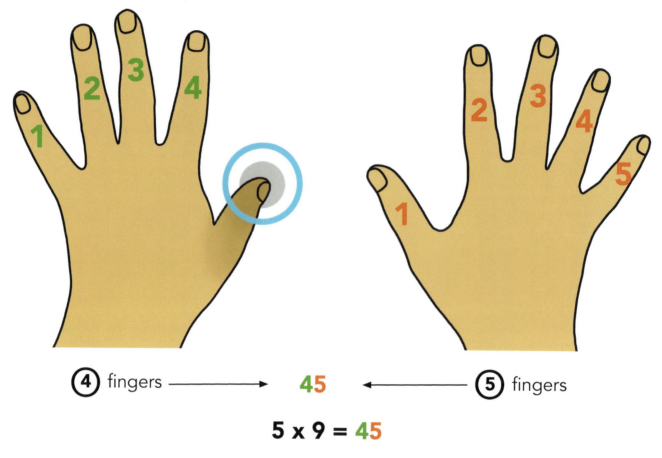

5 x 9 = 45

Your turn. Which time table calculation is that?

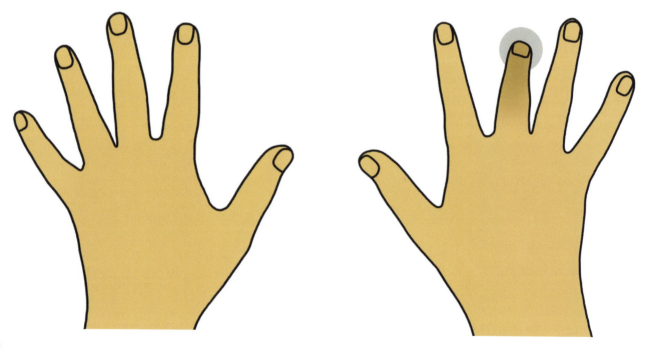

It's the **eighth finger** that is pressed down, so it must be **8** x 9.

There are seven fingers (**7**) BEFORE the pressed down finger, and two fingers (**2**) AFTER it.

$$8 \times 9 = 72$$

Looks and sounds easy? I bet it does. Now it's your turn to randomly test yourself in the x 9 table using your fingers.

> So far, we've been busy using **fingers** to find reference points that are the x 2, x 5, x 10 tables, and then work out 'on the spot' the x 6, x 7, x 8 and x 9 tables.
>
> In the following sections, you'll be invited to have a closer look at **patterns** that can be found inside the times tables. These patterns will make it easier to recall a whole table, for example 1 x 7 through to 10 x 7 by using pen and paper, your hand palm, or your imagination (the mind's eye). Practising quick recall of these patterns will help your brain make a really good sense of times tables so you won't forget them.

Turn 'times 2' into 'two lots of'
x 2

The x 2 table is one of the easiest, but if you ever get stuck, swap multiplication for addition. Simply **add the number to itself**.

$2 \times 2 = 2 + 2$ (two lots of 2)
$2 \times 3 = 3 + 3$ (two lots of 3)
$2 \times 6 = 6 + 6$ (two lots of 6)
$2 \times 8 = 8 + 8$ (two lots of 8)
$2 \times 12 = 12 + 12$ (two lots of 12)
$2 \times 15 = 15 + 15$ (two lots of 15)

and so on

Tic-tac-toe
x 3

Fill in a blank tic-tac-toe grid with 1-9 numbers, starting **from the bottom up**.

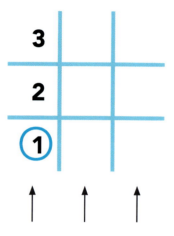

```
3 | 6 | 9
2 | 5 | 8
1 | 4 | 7
```

It's the bottom-up way because we're **building up** our x 3 grid.

Now give the grid levels 0, 1 and 2 (in the opposite direction to building the grid up - they are just levels).

```
0 →  3 | 6 | 9
1 →  2 | 5 | 8
2 →  1 | 4 | 7
```

```
03 | 06 | 09
12 | 15 | 18
21 | 24 | 27
```

Our x 3 grid is ready.

1 x **3** = **3**
2 x **3** = **6**
3 x **3** = **9**
4 x **3** = **12**
5 x **3** = **15**   and so on

The x 3 tic-tac-toe grid can be easily imagined (use your mind's eye) on your palm.

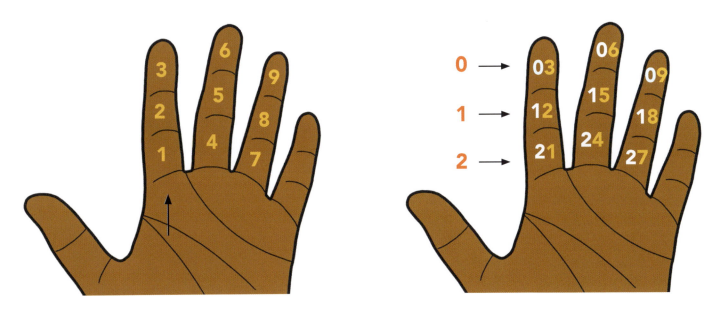

Now practise 'seeing' the x 3 tables by combining the numbers (1-9) together with the correct level numbers. Notice that **5** is in the middle of your palm grid.

What is **3 x 7**? Skip across your fingers' pads **7 times**. You have landed on number 1 with a level 2, which makes it **21**.

2, 4, 6, 8 Mountains
x 4

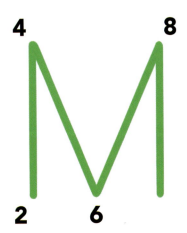

The M grid looks like two mountains joined together. We will number the grid's points: **2, 4, 6 and 8**, starting from the bottom. We have used **four** numbers because we are learning the **x 4** table patterns.

The last point on the grid has no number (for now).

Time to start adding levels.

0 ⟶ **04**   **08**

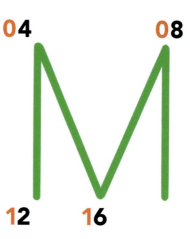

1 ⟶ **12**   **16**

Carry on adding levels, each time higher than the previous one.

2 ⟶ **24**   **28**

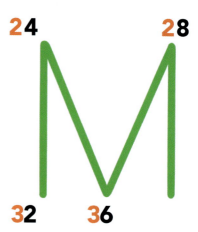

3 ⟶ **32**   **36**

Have you spotted any pattern yet? Read the values across the M grids, starting from the top.

04, 08, 12, 16...   We have created the x 4 times table.

1 x 4 = **4**
2 x 4 = **8**
3 x 4 = **12**
4 x 4 = **16**
5 x 4 = we already know it's **20**. Now write 20 under 08 on the grid.
6 x 4 = **24**
7 x 4 = **28**
8 x 4 = **32**
9 x 4 = **36**
10 x 4 = we already know it's **40**. Now write 40 under 28 on the grid.

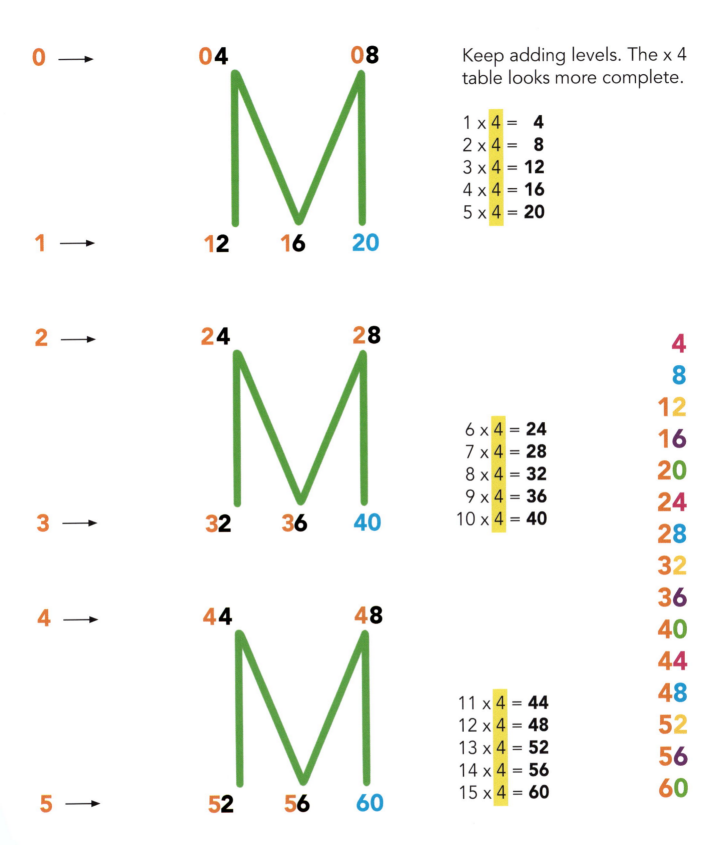

Keep adding levels. The x 4 table looks more complete.

1 x 4 = 4
2 x 4 = 8
3 x 4 = 12
4 x 4 = 16
5 x 4 = 20

6 x 4 = 24
7 x 4 = 28
8 x 4 = 32
9 x 4 = 36
10 x 4 = 40

11 x 4 = 44
12 x 4 = 48
13 x 4 = 52
14 x 4 = 56
15 x 4 = 60

Notice that all the x 4 table facts end in the very same digits we used to reference the M grid (2, 4, 6 and 8) and 0.
Numbers have an uncanny way of creating patterns.

Diamond tic-tac-toe
x 6

Did you know that the x 6 table is hiding inside the x 3 one?
That's why we will start with the tic-tac-toe method we used for the x 3 table.

	3	6	9
0			
1 →	2	5	8
2 →	1	4	7

03	06	09
12	15	18
21	24	27

The pattern for the x 6 table emerges when we draw a diamond in the middle.
The diamond connects four numbers on the grid.

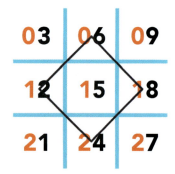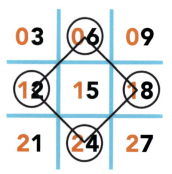

All you have to do to know your x 6 table facts is to read out the circled numbers:

1 x 6 = 6
2 x 6 = 12
3 x 6 = 18
4 x 6 = 24

Keep adding levels until the x 6 table is complete.

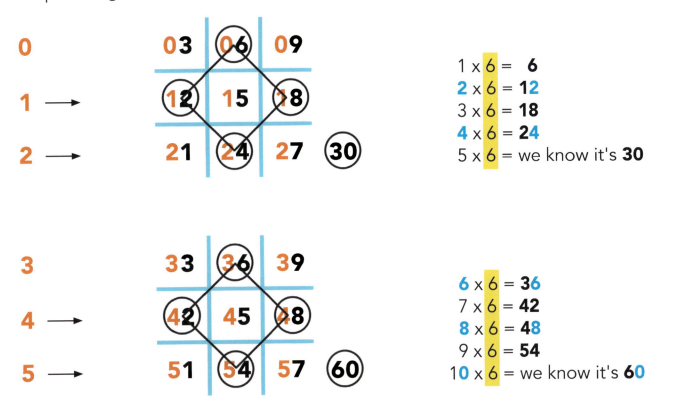

1 x 6 = 6
2 x 6 = 12
3 x 6 = 18
4 x 6 = 24
5 x 6 = we know it's 30

6 x 6 = 36
7 x 6 = 42
8 x 6 = 48
9 x 6 = 54
10 x 6 = we know it's 60

As with the x 3 table, you can imagine the diamond on the tic-tac-toe grid on your palm.

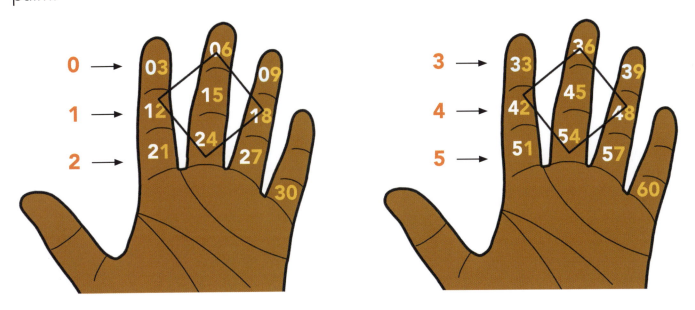

Remind yourself how you found the x 3 table on your palm (see page 15). Now practise finding the diamond on your palm for the x 6 table.

For **4 x 6**, follow the diamond pattern **4 times**. You have landed on **24**. 4 x 6 = 24

Upside-down tic-tac-toe
x 7

What if we turned the x 3 tic-tac-toe grid upside down? Well, this would happen...

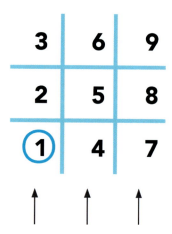

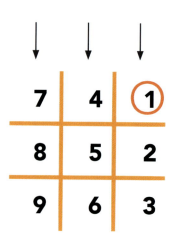

This is our x 7 **upside-down** tic-tac-toe grid. In future, to check yours is correct, make **7** the first number on the grid -- after all, this is the x 7 table.

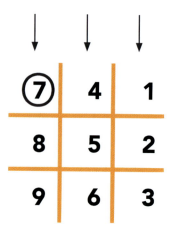

After the shaky upside down move, the grid's levels became **staggered (zig-zaggy)**.

0, 1, 2 → | 07 | 14 | 21 |
2, 3, 4 → | 28 | 35 | 42 |
4, 5, 6 → | 49 | 56 | 63 | 70

and so on...

1 x 7 = 7
2 x 7 = 14
3 x 7 = 21
4 x 7 = 28
5 x 7 = 35
6 x 7 = 42
7 x 7 = 49
8 x 7 = 56
9 x 7 = 63
10 x 7 = we know it's 70

Down in 1s, up in 2s
x 8

How is this down-up sequence created?
What are the patterns?

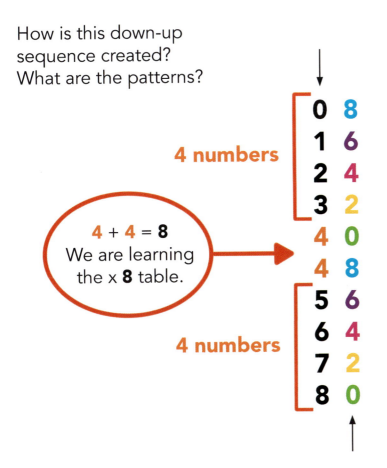

4 + 4 = 8
We are learning the x 8 table.

The first string of digits goes down in counts of 1.

After the first four digits, number 4 is repeated, and followed by another four digits in counts of 1.

So the pattern is:

4 numbers (0, 1, 2, 3)
4 and 4
4 numbers (5, 6, 7, 8)

In the second string of digits, we start at the bottom and count in 2s from 0. The pattern is repeated twice.

The 'Down in 1s, up in 2s' method gave us a perfect x 8 table.

1 x 8 = **8**
2 x 8 = **16**
3 x 8 = **24**
4 x 8 = **32**
5 x 8 = **40**
6 x 8 = **48**
7 x 8 = **56**
8 x 8 = **64**
9 x 8 = **72**
10 x 8 = **80**

For some people, it's easier to remember the pattern when it's in a box.

08	16	24	32	40
48	56	64	72	80

Notice the descending (from big to small) order of the UNITS: **8, 6, 4, 2, 0**.

We count the TENS from top left to botton right starting with 0. Our two 4s mark the end of the first line and the start of the new one.

Down in 1s, up in 1s
x 9

The x 9 table has the SIMPLEST down-up sequence ever.

0-9 down,
then
0-9 up.
Done!

1 x 9 = 9
2 x 9 = 18
3 x 9 = 27
4 x 9 = 36
5 x 9 = 45
6 x 9 = 54
7 x 9 = 63
8 x 9 = 72
9 x 9 = 81
10 x 9 = 90

↓
0 9
1 8
2 7
3 6
4 5
5 4
6 3
7 2
8 1
9 0
↑

Repeat or squeeze in the sum
x 11

For numbers 1-9, we simply **write the same number twice**.

1 x 11 = 11
2 x 11 = 22
3 x 11 = 33
4 x 11 = 44
5 x 11 = 55
6 x 11 = 66
7 x 11 = 77
8 x 11 = 88
9 x 11 = 99

For numbers greater than 9, we **squeeze in the two numbers' sum**.

10 x 11

10
↙ ↘
1   0

1 + 0
↘↙
1 1 0

10 x 11 = 110

12 x 11

12
↙ ↘
1   2

1 + 2
↘↙
1 3 2

12 x 11 = 132

34 x 11

34
↙ ↘
3   4

3 + 4
↘↙
3 7 4

34 x 11 = 374

23

If the sum of the two numbers is greater than 9, we carry and add the ten(s) to the left.

How easy was that!

Skip 5, skip 11
x 12

Here's another down-up sequence.
This time for the x 12 table,
where we **skip 5 and 11**
on the way down.

How to remember
5 and **11**?

Here's a little poem:

**Five eleven,
five eleven,
twelve times** missing
from the heaven.

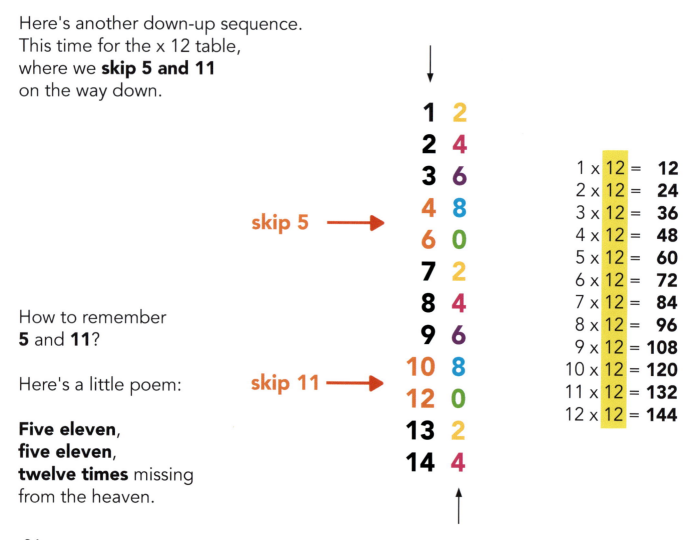

Line multiplication method

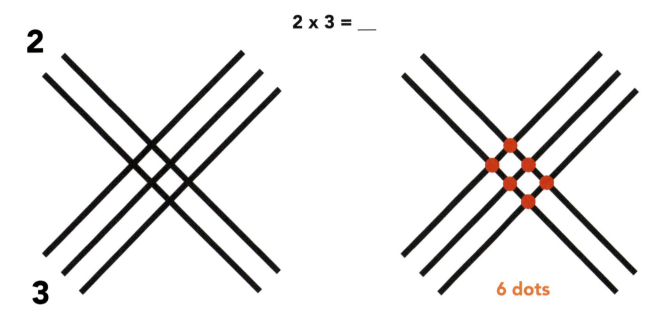

On a piece of paper, draw 2 lines by 3 lines diagonally.
Now count the number of junctions (the red dots on the drawing).

2 x 3 = 6

The larger the number, the more dot counting.

3 x 4 = __

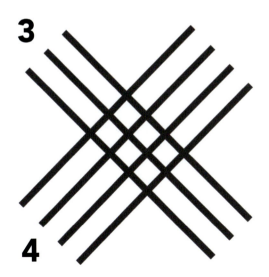 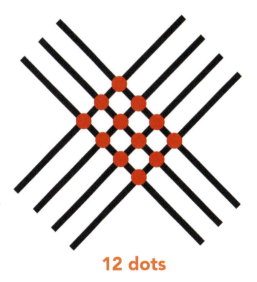

3 x 4 = 12

That's why this method works best for multiplying smaller 2-digit numbers.

11 x 21 = ___

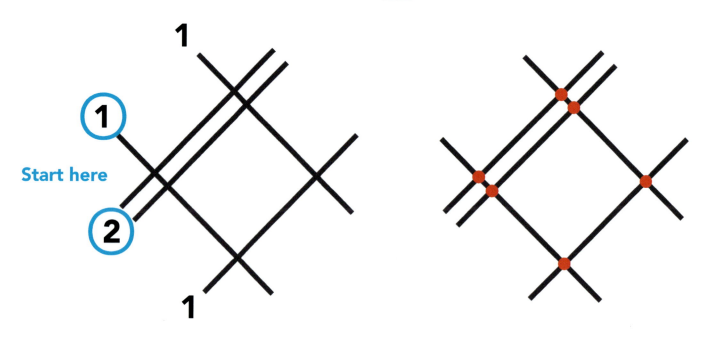

Start writing the numbers on the **left** side of your line drawing.
11 x 21 is not the same as 11 x 12.

Draw a curved line on each side, separating the left and right dot groups.
Circle the dots in the middle.

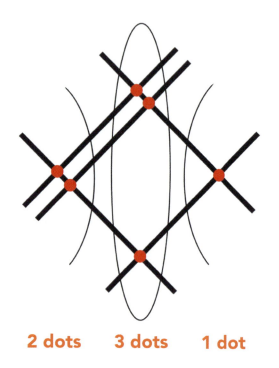

Count the number of dots in each area.

There are **2** dots, **3** dots and **1** dot.

11 x 21 = 231

2 dots   3 dots   1 dot

Let's try another example. But is it 21 x 12 or 12 x 12? Start your lines from the left.

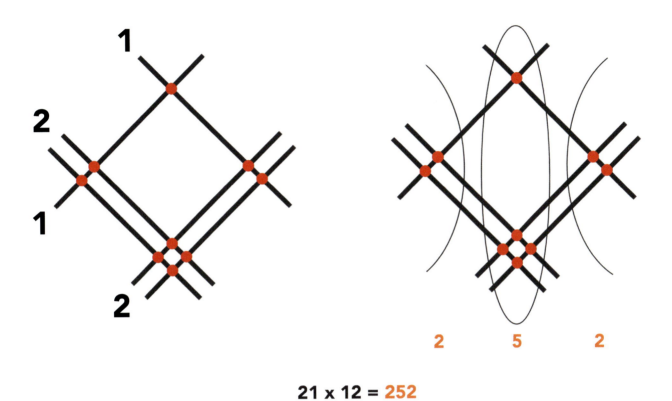

21 x 12 = 252

Your turn. What multiplication is drawn below? What's the answer?

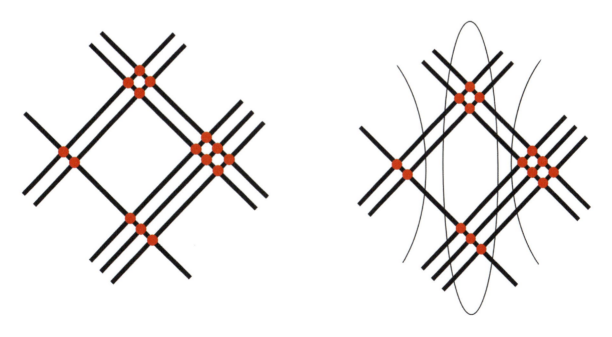

Check your answer on page 36.

We can use the same method for 3-digit numbers.

231 x 121 = ____

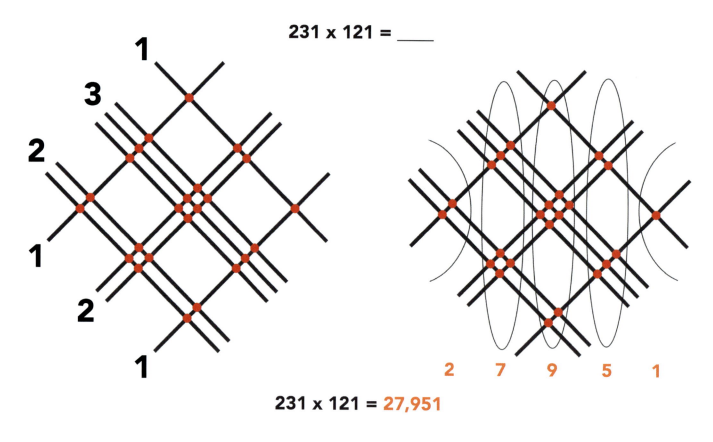

231 x 121 = 27,951

Your turn. What multiplications are drawn below? What are the answers?

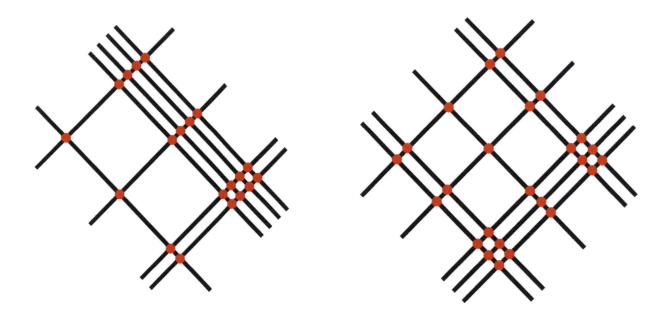

Check your answers on page 36.

When the dot number is greater than 9, carry and add the ten(s) to the left.

24 x 231 = ____

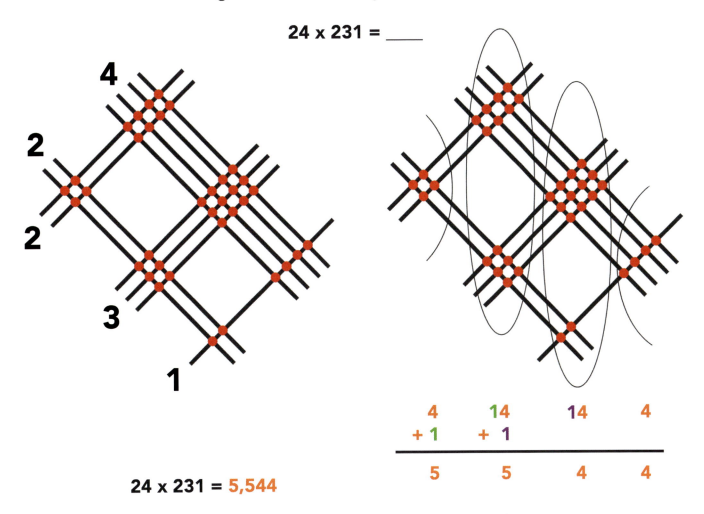

24 x 231 = 5,544

Your turn. What multiplications are drawn below? What are the answers?

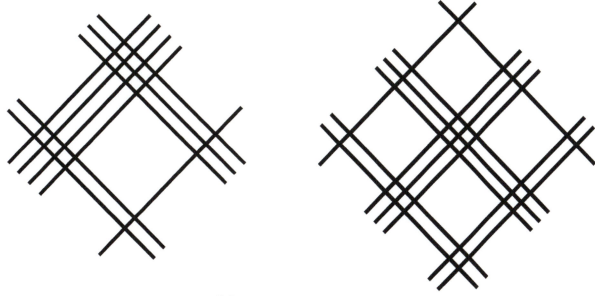

Check your answers on page 36.

321 x 201 = ___

If any digit is 0, draw a dotted line and don't count its junctions.

No red dots on the dotted line.

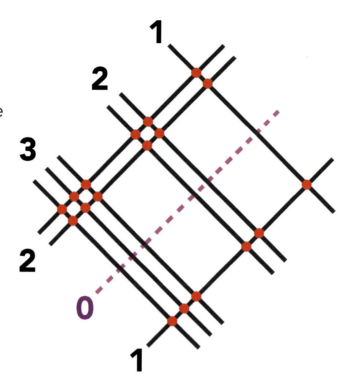

How many dots are there in each circled group of numbers?

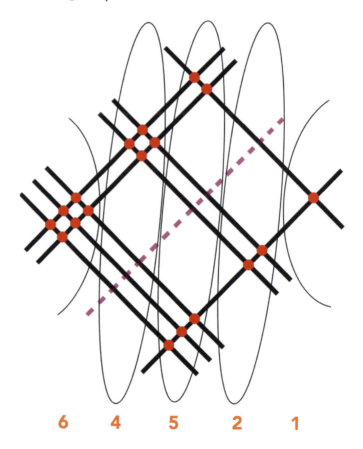

6   4   5   2   1

321 x 201 = 64,521

Your turn. What multiplications are drawn below? What are the answers?

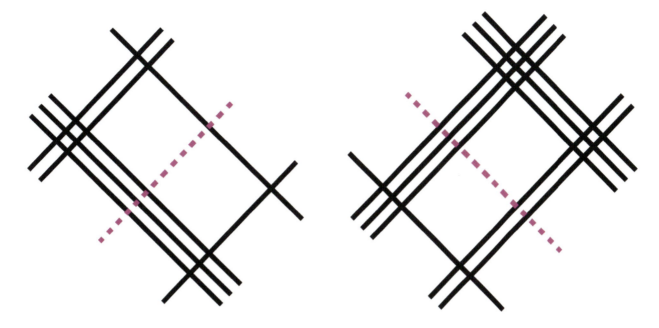

Check your answers on page 36.

Now come up with your own multiplications and practise the lines method on paper.

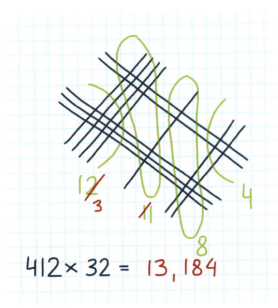

412 × 32 = 13,184

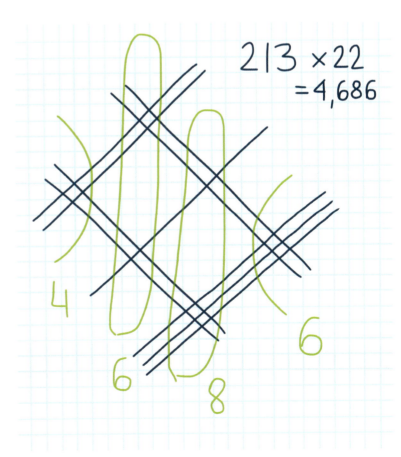

213 × 22 = 4,686

31

Lattice multiplication method

13 x 24 = ____

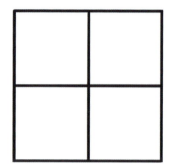

On a piece of paper, draw a box with four squares.

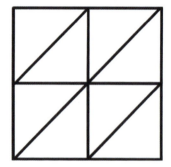

Now draw diagonal lines through the squares.

Your lattice template is ready.

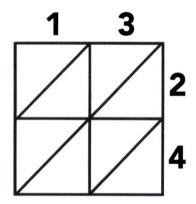

Put the numbers on the top and right sides of the box.

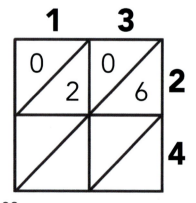

Starting with the top left-hand square, write down the result for 1 x 2 = 2, which will appear as 02, as both half-fields need completing. Then move on to calculate 3 x 2 = 6, which will appear as 06.

Now complete the entire box.
1 x 4 = 4, write 04.
3 x 4 = 12, write 12.

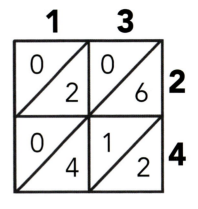

Sum up the digits in each diagonal, starting with the bottom right one.

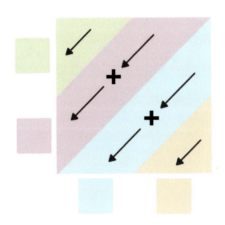
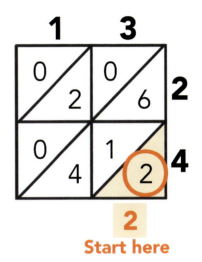

2
Start here

Read off the answer starting from the top, going down towards bottom right.

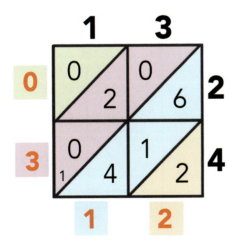
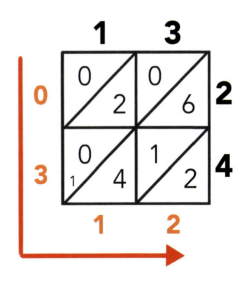

If any sum is greater than 9, carry and add the ten(s) to the left/up.

13 x 24 = 312

33

For larger numbers, you will need more squares.

23 x 164 = ____

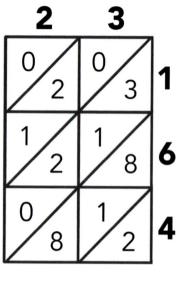

23 x 164 = 3,772

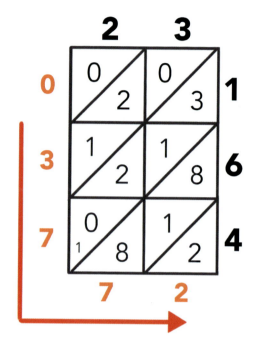

315 x 742 = ____

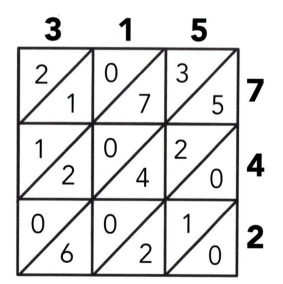

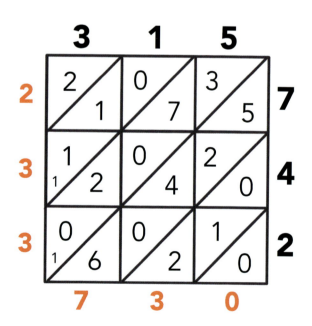

315 x 742 = 233,730

Your turn. Complete these multiplications.

31 x 45 = ____

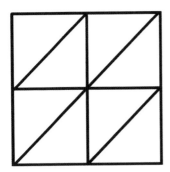

18 x 23 = ____

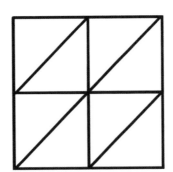

26 x 117 = ____

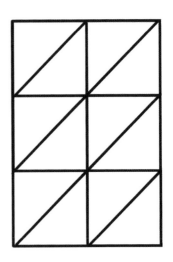

311 x 192 = ____

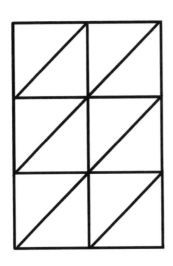

358 x 197 = ____

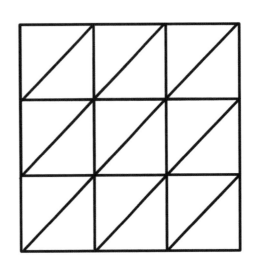

Now come up with your own examples and practise the Lattice method on paper.

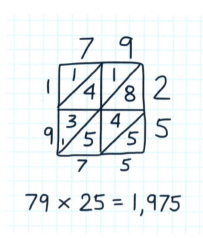

79 × 25 = 1,975

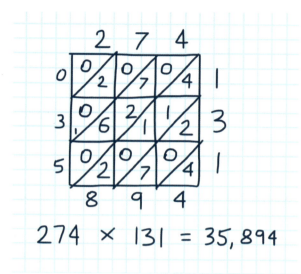

274 × 131 = 35,894

Answer key

Page 27: 12 x 23 = 276

Page 28: 112 x 14 = 1,568   113 x 212 = 23,956

Page 29: 41 x 23 = 943   132 x 231 = 30,492

Page 31: 201 x 31 = 6,231   32 x 103 = 3,296